What's Done In This House

Healing & Deliverance From Abuse

Deidra Saddler

What's Done In This House

Copyright © 2015 by DEIDRA SADDLER

All rights reserved. No part of this publication may be reproduced, stored in a retrieval system, or transmitted by any means – electronic, mechanical, photographic (photocopying), recording, or otherwise – without prior permission in writing from the author.

Unless otherwise noted, all Scripture quotations are from the New King James Version of the Bible Copyright © 1982 by Thomas Nelson, Inc. Used by permission. All rights reserved. http://www.nelsonbibles.com/

Scripture quotations marked "AMP" are taken from the Amplified® Bible, Copyright © 1954, 1958, 1962, 1964, 1965, 1987 by The Lockman Foundation. Used by permission. www.Lockman.org

Scripture quotations marked (NIV) are taken from the Holy Bible, New International Version®, NIV®.

Copyright © 1973, 1978, 1984 by Biblica, Inc. ™

Used by permission of Zondervan. All rights reserved worldwide. http://www.zondervan.com

Scripture quotations marked "MSG" or "The Message" are taken from The Message. Copyright 1993, 1994, 1995, 1996, 2000, 2001, 2002. Used by permission of NavPress Publishing Group. http://www.navpress.com/

Published in United States of America by Faith Walk Publishing LLC

Learn more information at: www.faithwalkpublishing.com

ISBN: 978-0-9905163-2-3

First Edition: August 2015

10 9 8 7 6 5 4 3 2 1

Dedication

This book is dedicated to all who have suffered some form of abuse at the hands of loved ones, those professing to love you, the unknown stranger, and even acquaintances. To every man, woman and child who has had their spiritual and emotional growth stunted by the circumstances surrounding an abusive encounter, whether physical, verbal, emotional, or financial. It is my sincerest hope that the words within the pages of this book will aid in the healing that is needed both spiritually and emotionally. That all who read will see that there is hope on the other side of pain and trauma; and be led by the Holy Spirit into the realization of the TRUTH that stands in the knowledge of God the Father being ONE who does love you with HIS ALL. Read and BE HOPED into A BLESS FILLED LIFE.

To my CHILDREN: Eric, Ramon, Treshawnda and Martece, to my Blessings in disguise the GRANDS: Malachi, Tayjuan, Taniah, Tyquez, Taviar, Kayla, Rachel, and Nariah, my sisters Devette, Danielle and Damara and my nieces and nephews, My MOMMA –Myrtis and my DADDY-Booker and ALL of the EXTENDED FAMILY--- I LOVE YOU WITH AN EVERLASTING LOVE that has NO

STRINGS attached and DOES NOT require you to prove it through conditions. May GOD heal all wounds from your past that have been suffered through abuse so that your feet may walk FREELY upon the paths of DESTINY etched out before time for YOU ALL to embrace.

Table of Contents

Dedication iii
Table of Contents v
Introduction 1
The Setup (Sexual Abuse) 3
Sticks and Stones (Verbal Abuse) 11
No Value No Respect (Emotional) 15
The Shadow of Death (Physical) 23
Insufficient Love (Financial) 28
Dry Bones 31
Hide & Seek 37
Scales Off-Ears Unplugged 42
Healing Wings 49
Clean House 59
Arise In Victory 64
About the Author 66
More From Faith Walk Publishing 67

Introduction

We have all heard it. Many of us have in our adulthood repeated it. "What's done in this house – stays in this house!" But what I have come to learn is this deliverance-blocking motto has caused many deaths- physically, emotionally, and spiritually. It has ripped relationships apart between mothers and daughters, and fathers and sons, and siblings too. This over rehearsed statement allows the enemy's goal to succeed, that being unhealed layers of scarring because of stifling years of unaddressed abuse.

This book was written for the sole purpose of allowing the abused to release the hurt. My primary goal was to write in a way that causes identification that leads to expression, then careful examination, then liberating healing and finally release. At the end of this healing process I want the injured to be able to take back the power that the abuse stole. The enemy can only use what we give him, and he only has the power of shame over us if we keep things hidden. If we open up, then the sting loses its power. We take away the enemy's grip when we use our experiences as testimonial stepping stones to freedom. This act of proclamation will allow us to remain free while simultaneously unlocking the prison doors for others, who have either experienced what we have in the past, or may be experiencing what we have right now in their present. Deliverance is the children's bread and it's time we came to the feast.

The Setup (Sexual Abuse)

"Now when she had brought them to him to eat, he took hold of her and said to her, "Come, lie with me, my sister." But she answered him, "No my brother, do not force me for no such thing should be done in Israel, Do not this disgraceful thing!" And I, where could I take my shame?... However, he would not heed her voice; and being stronger than she, he forced her and lay with her."

2 Samuel 13:11-14

"It happened to you too?" This was the beginning of a startling revelation that sexual abuse had hit my immediate family in multiple ways and through multiple people. Looking back on that day when my sisters and I began to share the darkest moments in our lives, it occurred to me that secrets will allow all sorts of heart damaging events to happen. Dark secrets that are tightly kept under lock and key by an all too familiar saying, "What's done in this house – stays in this house!" This deliverance-blocking motto has caused many deaths-

physically, emotionally, and spiritually. It has ripped relationships apart between mothers and daughters, and fathers and sons, and siblings too. This over rehearsed statement allows the enemy's goal to succeed of unhealed layers of scarring because of stifling years of unaddressed abuse.

Enter this book. For me this book represents God's hand reaching into the deepest, most hidden places of my soul and pulling out the cancerous root to many of my fears. He said, "What was done in this house doesn't have to stay in this house." and as I commit to move past the stagnation caused by focusing on the fear that writing this book would make certain people look really bad and ugly, I decided to center the attention instead on the healing and deliverance that could be received not only by me, but millions of others who have out of some fear of one thing or another chosen not to say a word about the things that were done in their houses, those both made of brick and blood.

Within this book names won't be used but certain situations will be highlighted so that the wounded that are reading this book may be able to see them self, and allow the healing that God wants to desperately give, and that they want desperately to receive- to come.

In Hollywood movies and television shows we have become familiar with the face of the molesting "Father", "Uncle", or "Male" friend of the family. But what if the one to force you into your first sexual encounter is of the same sex? What type of emotional and psychological damage is done then? Some may say, if the victim was female and there was no penetration not much, right? Wrong. The setup for this as well as any sexual abuse that is done within a child's developing stages is to cause an early arousal of sexual exploration and gender confusion, as it was in my case.

My first sexual abuse encounter was with an older female cousin when I was around 10 years old. Deliverance training on this subject has revealed that the enemy preys on children of any age, but the age range that is most susceptible to confusion in sexual orientation is from 10-13 years of age. The enemy sends spirits of perversion to take advantage of the abuse by beginning the gradual seduction of the child into promiscuity, homosexuality or lesbianism. I was bombarded with the following whispers after my first encounter;

"Certain things that she had you to do felt rather good didn't it?'

"What if you go and try it on your own terms"

"Are you sure that you aren't attracted to girls? Because your body responded to her in a pleasurable manner."

I want to interject something here- that will break the bondage of **shame** off the lives of you who were victims of sexual abuse rather the abuser were male or female. Your body responded favorably because that is what it was designed to do. God created sex to be pleasurable. He did not create it to be used in a perverted or abusive manner. Your body does not distinguish at the time of an assault that this is an assault "DON'T REACT", as you would if it were consensual. To the body sex is sex and sex is supposed to bring delight. Now that I have set that record straight let's move on.

When my second encounter of molestation took place at the hands of an uncle. I had dealt silently with the thoughts mentioned above for years. Fear came coupled with a whole new set of questions tied in shame to add to my personal battle of guilt. He did not penetrate me with his genitalia, however the fear I felt that night lying in the bed after being awakened as he fondled me both on the outside and inside of my body was just as stifling as one who had quote unquote gone all the way. When I finally talked myself into moving a bit, he then abruptly stopped and began to apologize for what he was about to do, which indicated to me he had planned to indeed go further than mere fondling. The ordeal ended of course with;

"Don't tell okay, I'm sorry, it won't happen again."

So I didn't tell. Why? Perhaps I didn't want to upset my father and mother, aunts or grandmother. Or maybe I believed that he would not try it again. He didn't at least not with me. It could have been self-preservation because I thought no one would believe me. But the reason that stands out the most to me as I write this is the same reason I never told anyone about that female cousin, because the enemy had placed the deceiving seed of- *"If you tell you are going to get into trouble for letting me do it."* **Letting her do it?** This is the lie that the enemy uses against victims of sexual abuse every time they are assaulted. *"You let them do it." "Or you invited it."* I was 10 years old I had no idea what sex was, and she was bigger and older a teenager in fact. At whatever age this may have happened to you know this **TRUTH<u>: you did not let them do anything, nor did you invite it to be done</u>.** It was their flesh coupled with demonic intent to change your destiny in GOD. Take the guilt off of you and place it where it belongs on the one who allowed themselves to be used as instruments of the enemy against you. I must interject a thought here. I say place it on the individual that allowed themselves to be used because rather we want to admit it, we the human race have a choice in the manner of rather or not we will allow our bodies to be used as tools of evil. Often times the abuser is older and stronger than the victim and has the power of submission via bullying or persuasion, it was **NOT, and I repeat NOT** your fault. At the time in my life when this second assault occurred I was a teenager. It was not words of accusation from his voice that stifled my tongue but instead accusations from my own thoughts that kept my mouth shut.

This time the following questions bombard me;

"Now just before you woke up you were beginning to respond very agreeably, so you liked what he was doing didn't you?"

"Why did you lay there pretending to be sleep it wasn't out of fear, you let him do it, you enjoyed it!"

"You aren't as innocent as you claim to be- you knew that was your uncle touching you."

"So which do you prefer the way a woman makes you feel or a man?"

Because of questions like these and many others set against me, I not only kept the *"don't tell"* rule, I also became determined to prove that I was solely heterosexual, and that I did not want nor desire the advances of my uncle. How? At the age of 14, I became promiscuous. Now in my mind I was only having sex with my boyfriend that is until I reached the age of 18. Looking back I found that I had from the ages of 14-26, nine boyfriends and this number did not include the one night stands, the group encounter, or my ex-husband that I married at age 29. There was a point in my life that the number of men I had given myself to sexually had exceeded my age. I had become totally consumed by the idea of proving that I was not a lesbian, and that I did wholeheartedly prefer men over women. The number of men solidified for me that I had healthy outside preferences and that I was not a nasty little pervert who enjoyed the advances of her uncle. However, what got lost in the process of proof, was who I really was according to God, and what He had planned for me.

By the age of 16, I had no sense of value for the person of me. Because like the woman in the opening scripture I had nowhere to take my shame, so I tucked it inside. Weighed with the guilt of shame I entered into a new arena of abuse, sometimes I quietly received it and at other times I gave it right back. This new field I found had more power than I had been led as a child to believe. It possesses the ability to stunt the progress of entire lives. This type lasted a lot longer than the bruises of physical abuse, and in most cases caused more psychological damage. It was almost an art-form or at least it became one to me. And when I learned the craftiness of it I used it with just as much detrimental precision as it was given to me. What was it? The destructively ravaging power of verbal abuse.

Sticks and Stones
(Verbal Abuse)

"Then he went up from there to Bethel; and as he was going up the road, some youths came from the city and mocked him," Go up, you baldhead! Go up, you baldhead!"

2 Kings 2:23

I know you may be wondering why I titled a chapter on verbal abuse "Sticks and Stones." Well, it has derived from the well-known and widely taught nursery rhyme that is a lie straight from the pit of hell.

"Sticks and stones may break my bones, but words will never hurt me."

Now you may say that's a bit harsh, it's just a little harmless saying to help children get over being teased. In actuality, what it is- is an attempted cancellation, a cute little not so harmless saying that nullifies the Word of God.

"Death and life are in the power of the tongue and they that love it shall eat the fruit thereof." Proverbs 18:21

If words could never hurt, then why does God give scriptures warning us about what we say? In the 12th chapter of Matthew we are told, "For by thy words thou shalt be justified, and by thy words thou shalt be condemned." Haven't you ever spoken something that you sincerely wish you had not? But once the words leave your tongue the damage is done, and just as the scripture says by your words you have been condemned. Proverbs 13:3 says, "He that keepeth his mouth keepeth his life; but he that openeth wide his lips shall have destruction." Cyber-Bullying has been the catalyst that has launched many of our youth into suicide. The world is filled with men and women who suffer from various forms of arrested development all because of the damaging words of a parent, loved one, or even a teacher, who spoke the lies of the enemy over them.

Lies like:

"You will never amount to anything."

"You're just like your no-good momma or daddy."

"You aren't smart enough to do that, stick to something

that is attainable."

"You are worthless!"

"I wish I had never given birth to you!"

"You are so stupid!"

"You are just as dumb as can be!"

"You are ugly!"

"You are fat!"

"You are shaped funny!"

"You have a funny looking face!"

Words I found can be specifically crafted to produce the most heart wrenching pain imaginable. Words can cut deeper than any knife could, and when demonically designed they do one thing very well …..DESTROY your self-esteem.

"You are the mother of four children with two different men, NOBODY will EVER want to marry you! You've lost your shape, and are tired looking. I should have put you on the corner when I had the chance."

This was spoken over me by the father of three of my children.

"Nobody wants you, your father doesn't want you he only took you because your mother had a nervous breakdown, she didn't want you all either she <u>chose</u> to go crazy instead of caring for you all."

These soul wrenching words were uttered over me as a teenager by a stepparent.

"You belong to me, and I can say or do anything I desire to you"

The above statement was spoken by one of the fathers of my children.

I look around today and my heart breaks as I listen to the way teenage girls talk to one another, the way they allow teenage boys to talk to them. I ask Lord, why do they allow such abusive language to be directed at them? His response-

"For the same reasons that you allowed it to be spoken to you, fear of rejection, and they do not know their value."

No Value No Respect (Emotional)

"Then the LORD said to me, "Go again, love a woman who is loved by a lover and is committing adultery, just like the love of the LORD for the children of Israel, who look to other gods and love the raisin cakes of the pagans...So I brought her for myself for fifteen shekels of silver, and one and one half homers of barley. And I said to her, "You shall stay with me many days; you shall not play the harlot, nor shall you have a man-so, too will I be toward you."

Hosea 3:1-3

Nothing is more heartbreaking as the moment when one recognizes that, their declared love one either by birth, marriage or confession from their lips, has no respect or value for them. Where there is no respect or value the *"anything goes"* attitude is attached, and the darkest imaginations can become instant realities within the life of the one who has become devalued and disrespected.

He Loves Me….. *Not*

Many times circumstances cause us to find ourselves placed in situations where we are forced to live a life with someone who has no love or desire for us in a way that a husband should love his wife, or vice versa.

"When the Lord saw that Leah was unloved, He opened her womb… She said the Lord has looked on my affliction. Now therefore my husband will love me….. And she conceived again and bore a son…. And she conceived again and bore a son and said, "Now this time my husband will become attached to me, because I have borne him three sons." Genesis 29:31-32, 33-34

"I was not his first choice. In fact, he only married me because I became pregnant and my stepfather said that I could not remain in the home with my baby. Do you know how hard it is to capture the heart of a man whose heart is already won? He already had a son by her… the one he truly loved. I gave birth to four daughters trying to give him a son."

My mother spoke these desperately sad words about my father. She kept trying for a son, so that he would love her; but she found just as Leah did that babies don't cause the fathers of those babies to love you especially if it wasn't you they wanted in the first place. What she gained for her troubles was a heart desperate for love and admiration for her alone, what she is still struggling with at the time of the writing of this book 47 years later is the fact that she is a heartbroken woman who lived an emotionally wounded life with a man that, "did the right thing" in the eyes of society by stepping up to take responsibility in a situation that he helped to create, but it was the wrong solution for her emotional well-being.

Within this marriage before it ended in dissolution there was adultery, physical and verbal abuse, and sadly a mental breakdown that is still being suffered all because she was not who he really wanted to be with. Just like Leah, who was placed by her father within a loveless marriage so was my mother and not only did she pay a hefty emotional price so did we, as her daughters who grew older and became witnesses of a marriage that unraveled sometimes violently before our eyes.

"What makes you think that I would ever marry you?"

My heart broke into one million tiny little pieces as I heard these words spoken from the mouth of my oldest daughter's father. You see we had been separated for about 3 years and in that time, unbeknown to me he had conjured up a plan that involved me falling back in love with him, affording him the opportunity to then dump me. As he felt I had done to him years prior. His plan worked marvelously well. Why? Open doors. I had not closed his chapter in my life and secretly wondered often *"what if."* Whenever I was not satisfied within my relationships I would daydream back to the time when I first met him, and how he treated me then. If this is you cry out to the Lord, for there is some unaddressed pain that has stunted your emotions and if it is not healed will succeed in leading you into a world of hurt. The way he or she treated you back then is just that *back then*. As so appropriately put by my Pastor, (We must leave our BEHIND) them and the feelings they had for you have changed even if they tell you differently. Change is inevitable as we grow, we change. Because of my wounded-ness he was able to fool me right up until the day we were supposed to pick up the marriage license, and then I was blindsided with the above question. He had lost respect and value for me and treated me as such. Yet I had no clue, oh the signs were there, but my eyes were colored by past encounters of his professed affections. And I desperately wanted him to still love and want me. I didn't know it at the time, but I needed him to want me because without his love I was of no value, so I believed.

"I should have put you on the corner when I had the chance."

Like I said at the ending of chapter one, I had no value of the person of me. And in the beginning of this chapter I stated that when the one who professes to love you really has no respect for or value of you, all sorts of things become acceptable in their eyes to say and do to you. I really don't know at what time in my life the man who spoke these cruel words thought that he could have put me on the corner, but as I looked back over my life I realized that I had already put myself there metaphorically speaking. I had indeed whored myself out and for no price at all. It was done under the guise of;

"A woman has needs and just as much right as any man to have them satisfied."

Personal devaluation will allow you to believe the statement above is not only true, but is an acceptable form of conduct. It will also keep you in relationships where there is no love or respect.

"I knew I shouldn't have married you when I was standing at the altar."

These words were spoken to me by my ex-husband. He had become angry about my opening of a separate bank account because of his drug addiction. I stayed within a physically, verbally, emotionally and financially abusive marriage for 9 years and 9 months. Why? I told myself it was because I was waiting on God to heal it. Now part of that was true, a small part. But digging deeper I found that I was trying yet again to outlive a word curse spoken earlier in my life over me by one of the fathers of my children.

"You are the mother of four children with two different men, NOBODY will EVER want to marry you!"

You see I didn't realize it, but I had actually received this curse and had lived for years unconsciously believing that no one would want to marry me. The two of them hadn't as a matter of fact they both went on to marry other women and left me with our children. This substantiated the belief held by me that I was good enough to make babies with, but not good enough to marry. And so this marriage that I was within was the best that I could ever hope to have. As a matter of fact the mere fact that he had a drug addiction proved the theory that no-one in their *right mind* would ever want me. So what I needed to do was buckle down and, *wait* on the Lord to fix my situation. My hope lied within the multitudes of testimony that came into the church of women whose husbands were addicted to drugs, alcohol and even gambling and God healed their marriages and delivered their husbands. I believed wholeheartedly that I just needed to keep the faith, pray for him *and show God that our marriage deserved to be healed too. After all, I was a Christian now, no longer a whoremonger. I was having sex the legal way.*

Did you catch the last three sentences? Look at them again- this mentality is birthed out of the belief that God only values you when you are doing what is considered the right thing to do. When one is of this mindset, and healing and deliverance don't come in the way it has for others, they fall dangerously into the conviction that either,

A- God is punishing me for all the wrong I did before coming to Him.

Or

B- I don't have enough faith.

Or my personal belief at that time-

C-This is just my lot in life and I don't deserve better.

These beliefs totally negate truths like;

God's love and value of you is not predicated on your obedience to Him- because He died when the world was still in sin, That ***God doesn't punish people after conversion for sins committed before conversion,*** that ***God does not force***

healing and deliverance onto people they have to want it, and that *every choice has consequences that come with it* and they will come rather they are good or bad, and if they happen to be bad *it doesn't mean that God is mad at you for making the wrong choice and has decided to send hell fire and calamity into your life.*

But when you are emotionally scarred you do not realize that thinking opposite of what has been revealed above is a flawed way of thinking. When everyone that has ever uttered the words "*I LOVE YOU*" has also been the same people to hurt you the most, you don't know what **REAL LOVE** looks like. And when you are introduced to a religion and not a relationship with Jesus Christ it takes even that much longer for you to find out the TRUTH.

The Shadow of Death (Physical)

"When they had twisted a crown of thorns, they put it on His head, and a reed in His right hand. And they bowed the knee before Him and mocked Him, saying, "Hail, King of the Jews!" Then they spat on Him, and took the reed and struck Him on the head."

Matthew 27:29-30

"*You are going to have a black eye after this one for sure.*" Were the words I spoke to myself as I looked in the mirror while I wiped the blood from my mouth and nose, and carefully tended to the one eye that was swollen shut. This was the second or maybe third time that he had jumped on me because I caught him cheating. The first time happened when I was seven months pregnant with his second child. Devaluation of self has one to believe that any type of affection is love, (including lust) and in love you take the good and the bad. The bad may be you getting slapped around once in a while. Your job is to simply learn what not to say or do, to cause a fight.

I learned the above ideal from watching my mother, whenever she and my father would get into physical fights with each other- she merely fought back so I figured that is what you do. You fight back, but under no circumstances do you leave. I made excuses for his behavior, his mother beat him and his father abandoned him, and so he really doesn't know how to love. You would think that these revelations would have sent me running to the hills away from him, but instead it drew me closer. I had the ill-fated belief that I could teach him how to love.

Me, the one who didn't know how to love either, nor what love even looked like. I eventually left this situation not because he hit me, but because I got tired of catching him with other women who also wanted to fight me. But I didn't close the door on this relationship fully either because after leaving and having a child with someone else, single again, I went back to him when he said all the right things and had my fourth child. I was 21, a mother of four, and an emotional wreck. Longing for love and having no clue where to find it or how to give it to my children.

"I know you have some money hidden! I know you do and you are going to give it to me or you are not going to leave this room!"

My ex-husband spoke these words as he held a knife to my throat. I screamed for my teenage sons and cousin to go get help. They instead broke the door down to my bedroom and chased him out of the house. Those of you that have not experienced this type of abuse may ask the questions, *"Why doesn't she just leave?" "What is wrong with her?* Or mistakenly believe that- *she obviously likes being hit on!"* And even as I sit here and type these instances decades after living through them, the only answer that I can give you as to why I stayed even after that is – I was a damaged person. I had no worth in my eyes. I believed that because I had chosen to marry this man, that I was bound to accept whatever happened within our marriage.

"Ma'am, can you hear me? Ma'am, I need you to answer me. How many fingers do you see? What is your name? Do you know where you are?"

The paramedic asked while bending over me as I lay on the floor of my living room while he motioned to his partner to help him place me on the stretcher.

"We are taking your mother to the hospital, she has a concussion."

My youngest daughter stood by with tears in her eyes, my brother-in-law trying to console her.

"Keep an eye on her this weekend. If she seems disoriented or doesn't respond take her to the emergency room immediately."

The above words were spoken to my friends as I lay on the emergency room gurney groggily returning to consciousness after a concussion. This time the offender was my 15 year old son. He had tackled me after I disciplined him for speaking profanity at his younger sister. When I fell my head bounced off the linoleum floor in the bathroom, and then I was out. Where did he learn this treatment of me? From me. Now I am not condoning his behavior at all, and he for many, many weeks after begged for forgiveness. You see he had watched for five years, physical abuse bestowed upon me at the hands of my then husband. He had assumed since I didn't leave that this is the way a woman is supposed to be treated. That men, when angry about what has been said or done to them, react in this manner.

Now let's look deeper into why I didn't leave. How could I leave? Leaving meant admitting that I was indeed a failure, and not capable of keeping a husband. Leaving meant that his father was right, and I was unworthy of companionship. Leaving meant that I didn't have faith that God would fix it. No, I could not leave- God was going to intervene; I just had to wait it out. I was taught as a young girl that God hated divorce, and I had finally got on the right path with God by marrying and, I would not for any reason get off that path.

This may not sound logical and certainly was not in any means the correct way for me to believe that this is what God thought of me, nevertheless it was at that time my belief. I write this to say to you the wounded reading this book, don't beat yourself up for not getting out- for if you could have honestly you would have. But know this, abuse, physical or otherwise is not what God has for you, nor does He expect you to stay in a relationship while you are being abused, get out and get help especially if you have children who are witnessing this behavior.

For you who have not experienced this type of abuse, don't assume anything when it comes to the reasons why a person stays in this kind of an abusive relationship. The reasons are vast and complicated. It will take God's compassion, patience and wisdom to minister to such a one. Such a one needs God's healing for deep emotional hurt and deliverance from the Spirits of Rejection, Self-Hatred, Shame, and Arrested Development just to name a few.

Insufficient Love (Financial)

"But if anyone does not provide for his own, and especially for those of his household, he has denied the faith and is worse than an unbeliever."

1 Tim. 5:8

Rarely is the abuse one can suffer financially thought of as abusive. But it is exactly that if the financial hardship suffered is brought on at the hands of another, by either deliberate withdrawal of financial support or the toll that addictions bring in devastating waves as money from within the household is taken out to support a habit, of drugs, alcohol or gambling.

Mother's Day 2005 I attended a worship service in a small Florida town where I was residing. The speaker took the sacred desk and prayed with eyes that felt as though they were set directly upon me gave the title of her message, "When Helping You Is Hurting Me." Within her message she spoke of various ways that we go out of our way to help those who either flat out refuse to help themselves or refuse to acknowledge that they have a problem. Even if this problem is not only destroying them, but the entire family as a whole.

It was this sermon that opened the door for change to come into my life and the lives of my children because up until that moment I had not even thought about leaving. At that time in my life I was married to a man that refused to acknowledge that he had a drug addiction. His cocaine habit during the life of our nine year marriage succeeded in draining bank accounts, and caused mortgage, rent, utilities, and car payments to go unpaid.

During the times that he and I lived in the same home he did not work more than a month at a time, and by the time he received his second paycheck he was fired for absences due to drug induced binges. Our joint bank accounts were constantly overdrawn leaving the necessities of daily living un-provided for. There were countless paydays that our family did not get to take advantage of, because I would wake up and find the bankcard gone from my purse. Even money hidden within the house was found and used to feed the habit that was slowly killing his body and the fragile psyches of both mine and those of my four children.

It was the words within that sermon that caused me to see that if I continued to stay, my children and I would suffer possibly even greater than we had already. The next day I, and my youngest daughter who was 16 at the time went into a shelter for abused women. She was the only one of my four children who had returned home at this stage in my life. His assorted array of abuse and my woundedness had driven my other three children out of our home.

Dry Bones

"The hand of the Lord was upon me, and He brought me out in the Spirit of the Lord and set me down in the midst of the valley; and it was full of bones."

Ezekiel 37:1

So now my body was out, but my mind and emotions were still in captivity. In the shelter with other women who had managed to escape their personal lives of torture I wondered what exactly was to come of this very bold and scary first step. This particular shelter had mandatory counseling sessions that required group attendance. I don't believe that this setting was the best choice in dealing with women who for the most part kept their abusive situations hidden from outside eyes. I rarely spoke about the deep things that needed to be exposed. I spoke just enough to give the appearance of cooperation so that I would not lose my place in the shelter. Speakers were brought in to try and de-program our faulty thinking. You know, get to the root of why we entered into and stayed within the abusive relationships of our pasts and present circumstances.

It was within these group sessions that we were made to see the harsh reality of abuse that we had succumbed to. We learned what abuse was and what love wasn't. What we or I should say I did not learn within that six week stay there was, why? Why did I believe the lies put before me? Why did I believe that it was my lot in life to be treated that way? Why did I believe that I could not leave? And how I would begin to return to the land of the living beyond abuse?

Within that temporary place of solace I simply did what I had already been doing stuffing my emotions (*Dry Bones*) because they simply were not helpful to feel. Besides, I needed to get about the business of finding a job and an apartment for me and my daughter to live. We did only have six weeks to stay there, this place was a stepping off point, it was not intended nor were they going to allow it to be a landing pad. During my stay there a lot of hurt (*Dry Bones*) floated to the surface, but they were past issues as far as I was concerned and I had not the luxury to dwell on the past.

I left the shelter armed with some need to know information about abusive cycles and traps, but without any healing or deliverance for my damaged soul, heart and mind. I was merely existing there was no joy of life and my spirit was tightly locked away.

My daughter and I had begun to treat each other cordially, but that was the extent of our relationship. She had wounds that I had yet to learn about. She did not trust that I would keep her needs at the forefront of things that must be looked after, because frankly, I had not given her a tract record to believe that. She knew not of the reasons I stayed, or why I allowed them to stay in the mess that was my marriage, because I didn't know them. From her point of view, it was simple I had chosen him- over them, and the reason for her was clear cut, I stayed because I didn't want to be alone. It would take years for me to get them to understand the truth.

How does a mother begin to rebuild the fragile bond that is for most a given between a mother and a daughter? Where does she start? Should she apologize first for the intrusion brought by "I Do"? Or does she simply sweep the past and all of its jagged edged bones underneath the proverbial rug and hope beyond all hope that they can just start over?

Does she try to become her friend and forget about being a parent? Is she over compensating by allowing her rants and rages to go unchallenged? Dry bones- I read in the Word of God, "Can these bones live?" And I wondered if mine could?

I made a list in my mind of what had died within me. I will call them my Dry Bones List.

Dry Bones List

- *Faith in True Love*
- *Trust, especially in Men*
- *The ability to believe that life would get better*
- *Dreams*
- *Hope that my relationships with my children would be restored*
- *Hope that I would ever experience a loving marriage*
- *Faith that God had promises for me*
- *My Identity*

The enemy had returned, this time with spirits of depression and torment. Torment wasted not one day of whispering to me that I was alone now and would always be. I had missed my chance of God performing any miracles in my life because I had not stayed within the marriage long enough for Him to do what only He could. I had not stayed because I had no faith. I was told that the message that gave me the courage to leave was not a message from God and I was now out of His grace because I had gotten a divorce and that He would never help me now.

The depression brought with it "Memory Recall", a constant reminder of past times of despair which opened the door wide for the, "spirits of Grief and Suicide." Yes, there is a spirit of grief it is not the normal grief that one feels within a loss of some kind. No this type of grief wields the captured with an inability to move forward within the natural stages of grief. This spirit links up with hopelessness and produces a chronic state of victimization within its subject. They in turn invite the "Spirits of Bitterness and Rejection," to take up residence which quickly began to plant deep inside the soul the poisonous seeds of bitter root expectations.

"Dry Bones."

It is a well-known fact within the body of believers who have been enlightened in the areas of healing and deliverance that demonic oppressions can manifest within the body as physical infirmities, sickness and disease. Within my body, Premature Death was given a wide entrance because of my spiritual state of oppression and illness became my portion. I began to suffer repeated bouts of pneumonia, bronchial infections, and then asthma. Obesity clung to my frame as I made food my only companion and trusted soother. I tried to bury myself in church activity and for a while it worked. My spirit trapped had a view of my soul that had gradually begun to look like the below passage;

"The hand of the Lord came upon me and brought me out in the Spirit of the Lord, and set me down in the midst of the valley; and it was full of bones. Then He caused me to pass by them all around, and behold, there were very many in the open valley; and indeed they were very dry." **Ezekiel 37:1-2**

Dry Bones that had successfully burrowed deep beneath my conscious mind and were operating without restraint in every area of my life. Physically, emotionally, financially, and spiritually I had become overcome with Dry Bones and I had no idea if they would ever be able to live.

Hide & Seek

"But the Israelites committed a trespass in regard to the devoted things; for Achan son of Carmi, the son of Zabdi, the son of Zerah, of the tribe of Judah, took some of the things devoted [for destruction]... Behold, they are hidden in the earth inside my tent, with the silver underneath."

Joshua 7:1a, 21b

Now before you decide to permanently close this book with red hot contempt of this scripture choice let me explain why I chose it. Trust me, I hear you saying abuse is not a trespass that the abused commits it is the abuser that is committing the trespass! Yes, and I agree. But the part of the scripture that I want to highlight here is, ***"took some of the things devoted for destruction."*** Many times the wounded take and keep the things that abuse has devoted for destruction within our lives. And our lives continue to go in a downward spiral often decades after the abuse has been suffered. In the last chapter I spoke that I was overcome with dry bones.

In every area of my life there was death. The reason is because I had kept the fruits of the abuses suffered, and buried them as Achan did with the treasures found that he had been commanded by God not to keep but destroy. ***"Behold, they are hidden in the earth inside my tent, with the silver underneath."***

You may now be asking of me, "Are you saying that we regard the condemning words, and ill-fated actions said and done to us as treasures of silver?" The answer is No. On the contrary, we despise these things and truly desire to be rid of them, but often because of the cloud of secrecy that we have been steeped within we have learned to simply bury them instead of releasing them via confessions. Sometimes the abuse was so traumatic in nature that we block it from conscious memory because that was the only way survival could have been ascertained. But God desires truth within our inward parts. And the only way for true healing and deliverance to be received is for us to face the demons of our past and allow God to cast them out.

***"Behold, You desire truth in the inward parts, And in the hidden part You will make me to know wisdom."* Psalm 51:6**

In order for this to be done, we may have to go on a journey of hide and seek. Within these soul searching expeditions we seek to find that which has become firmly embedded beneath the foundations of our belief systems. We have to search out the core causes of destructive cycles in our lives, the meaning behind areas of stagnation, and arrested development of character.

Remember how the last chapter ended. I had become deeply entangled with spirits of depression, suicide, premature death, grief, infirmity and bitterness. While all this and other things were going on the inside I on the outside put on a mask of happiness. I walked within a façade of peace and tried desperately to hide by immersion into church activity. I was a walking wounded clump of a being. Rejection ran from my pores. Fear blanketed me. I built walls to protect my walls to ensure that no one would get in as I simultaneously succeeded in keeping my spirit and all the darkness from being able to get out. I had become an unwilling resident of the kingdom of Deep Hurt. Just like you who are now reading this book have too.

It is time for you, the wounded in soul, in heart, in mind, and in spirit to take the hide and seek grand tour into the vast darkness that has held you within bondage and allow an excavation of light to occur. The Father is waiting to take away all that hinders you within the relationship that He desires to have with you. He is waiting to restore the shattered, broken shards of your heart that keep you from receiving His love and the love of others. He is ready to create within you a clean heart. To restore within you a sound mind. To help your soul to prosper as your health does. And to unlock the prison that keeps your spirit chained.

If you are ready to begin the exploration into your healing, then pray this prayer;

"Lord God, I come to you chained to the sorrows of the past. Some Lord, I am well aware of but there are some that have been buried so deep that I have forgotten them and it is these that are causing unforeseen calamity to reside within my life. I want to know the TRUTH. I want to be healed and not only healed, but made whole in YOU. I want wisdom so that I may renounce the lies that are attached to these deep hurts. The lies that I have believed about You, others, and myself. I yield today to the leading of your Holy Spirit, He whom you have sent to guide me into all truth. Father, I will not back out because it becomes too painful to see, but I will push through the pain of the event and receive my blessing of deliverance. Walk with me, Jesus, hold my hand as I travel in time to destinations where trespasses were first done against me. Hide me in Your Blood and keep me from the lies of the enemy as you reveal that which must come out. I surrender all and will receive the inheritance of deliverance which is my rightful possession. In Jesus name, Amen."

Special Note-

As The Father begins to reveal things about you argue not against them, with statements of *"that is not me"* or *" I haven't acted like that"* simply accept what He shows as true, then ask what action is He now requiring of you in respect to that which is being uncovered. For often God deals with our reaction to the offense before He can heal the heart of it. This next step is key in receiving the healing necessary- **OBEY** what He gives you to do. For faith without works is dead. You will not become free of the bondages of abuse if you do not do what He is advising you to do.

Scales Off-Ears Unplugged

"And at the end of the days [seven years], I, Nebuchadnezzar, lifted up my eyes to heaven, and my understanding and the right use of my mind returned to me; and I blessed the Most High [God] and I praised and honored and glorified Him Who lives forever, Whose dominion is an everlasting dominion; and His kingdom endures from generation to generation."

Daniel 4:34

I hear the bible scholars saying, this scripture is dealing with a King who had taken on the deity of God as himself. He had started taking credit for the things that God had done and had not honored God by giving Him the honor that was due Him alone. And they are correct. But I ask you to go a step further here with me and look at your life. You that have been wounded. Look at your mindset about God, have you blamed God for the pain in your past and possibly your present? In so doing have you decided that God is not to be praised for what- ever, if any good happens in your life? Have you taken the place of the LORD in your life? Making all decisions upon that which you think is right? Has your communication with the Father slowed or ceased altogether?

If you have answered yes to any of these questions, then I am compelled to inform you that you have taken the same stance as Nebuchadnezzar and because of this the eyes of your understanding have been clouded. The right use of your mind has taken a wrong turn and the realization of God is Most High worthy of honor, praise and glory have become dulled. And so because He has decided that this is the end of those times in your life He wants to restore unto you understanding. He wants to renew your mind by the grace of HIS BLOOD COVENANT, and reestablish for you the right use of it.

Now I am not so without apathy to understand why you may have wandered into the forsaken hills of a God no more. For I will admit that I have had some bouts myself with anger against God for that which I have suffered, but if you want to be healed from the tormenting pain that is a byproduct of abuses suffered then I must inform you; that God can no longer remain on the outside of your life and heart. For He is the only one who is able to give you freedom from the bondages of abuse in whatever form you have been unfortunate to experience them.

In the last chapter you prayed a prayer to allow God to excavate the needed areas of darkness within your soul. This chapter is the next step that will be taken by you. Indeed, your eyes and ears will be opened, so that you will not only see the offenders and their offenses, but your offenses as well.

Let me explain, you see when God starts His healing process within each of us He deals with **US** not the ones who have hurt us. He deals with our hurt, our reactions to the hurt, and the hurt that we have instilled upon others and against Him. So do not smash the mirror because the scales have fallen from your eyes. Do not choose to go deaf suddenly because your ears have been unplugged. As the Father begins to unfold you before you, take heed, for it is a needful thing in order for wholeness to be attained.

Remember the Dry Bones List from chapter six-

Dry Bones List

- *Faith in True Love*

- *Trust, especially in Men*

- *The ability to believe that life would get better*

- *Dreams*

- *Hope that my relationships with my children would be restored*

- *Hope that I would ever experience a loving marriage*

- *Faith that God had promises for me*

- *My Identity*

Well, it has been the items within this list and much more that God has had to deal with me during my times of "Scales off- Ears Unplugged", of which I am compelled to inform you will be an ongoing state. Why? Because The Father has appointed times of revelation due in part of the very real fact that we can't handle everything at once. During my times in this stage of healing I learned that I had no faith in true love, His Love. I had ascribed to the all familiar saying that "all men were dogs." I continually and unconsciously spoke death over my life circumstances. I had stopped writing altogether so the dream of being a writer had been thrown not placed on a dusty shelf somewhere in the cosmos. It was broken and marred and no longer looked like something that I had ever desired to do. I had falsely accepted that my relationship with my children would forever be one of hi and bye with limited ability for them to stand being in my presence anything longer than a week at best.

I had succumbed to the idea that my life would be lived out in a broken, miserable and abusive marriage, a loving marriage would never be my portion and because of all of this I was angry with God. My anger towards Him blocked all faith that He had any promises for me or that He desired to do anything for me, which translated for me the belief that I had to do for myself. I became independent, and self was not placed on the cross. I lived a surface salvation where Jesus was my Savior, but I was my LORD. To have Jesus as LORD means that HE is in total control of every aspect of your life. No decision is made in and of yourself. You have no answers. Your desires are those that He has placed within you and they correspond with the vision of the FATHER. Will you have a life? Yes, but it will be guided by HIS very best for you and not what you think the very best for you is.

So trust me when I say I understand that this chapter may be the least liked and possibly even a bit despised because it causes us to take a look at OUR FAULTS and not at the faults of those that have hurt us.

But God could not be seen as just if He only dealt with everyone else and never with the individual that has come to Him for help. Our healing would never reach a status of complete because we would miss the biggest blockage to obtaining the freedom we want by skipping over dealing with SELF.

God is kind. He does not beat us over the head with our faults and misgivings. He speaks in gentle tones not harshly in fire and brimstone styled condemnation. That voice is the enemy. The Father's voice is coated with conviction which leads us to repentance. We see our faults as He does and then choose to turn away from the behavior towards the TRUTH.

As painful as this step in the journey may be, it is also the most liberating. When you allow it to do what it is meant to do, you step out of the old you that is bogged down in guilt, shame, anger, resentments, fear, rejection and other poisonous fruits of the enemy into the new creation that receiving salvation gave you. Identity is restored. Joy is received. Love is swallowed up by you in huge doses. . You are able to receive and give the love of GOD to others. Courage becomes your new style of dress. You are no longer guarded by fear. Your real personality begins to shine. Creativity begins to flow from God through you. Peace is your portion no matter what the circumstances are.

Doesn't the opportunity to gain all that make the short moments in time that you will have to face you worth it?

Good, I'm glad that you agree. So it's mirror time. This must be done in a quiet atmosphere for you must allow yourself to hear what God reveals. So go to a room where you can be alone if you have a family, put a sign on the door that says, *"Private Session With Jesus Do NOT DISTURB."* If you can go on a weekend or day excursions devoted to facing you do that. I recommend a visit to a phenomenal spiritual place called *"THE SANCTUARY"* located in Whitewater, Wisconsin, owned by a powerful woman of God, Apostle Pernell Hewing operated solely by the Holy Spirit. If you can get away for 3 or more days look this place up on the internet and follow the instructions given when you arrive you will be placed in the room that GOD has a need for you to be in order to deal with whatever He chooses in you at that time in your life. Pray and then wait, He will respond.

"This is the agreement (testament, covenant) that I will set up and conclude with them after those days, says the Lord: I will imprint My laws upon their hearts, and I will inscribe them on their minds (on their inmost thoughts and understanding), He then goes on to say, And their sins and their law-breaking I will remember no more." **Hebrews 10:16-17**

Healing Wings

"But unto you who revere and worshipfully fear My name shall the Sun of Righteousness arise with healing in His wings and His beams, and you shall go forth and gambol like calves [released] from the stall and leap for joy."

Malachi 4:2

Remember the below passage from a previous chapter; *"Depression brought with it "Memory Recall", a constant reminder of a past time of despair which opened the door wide for the, "spirits of Grief and Suicide." Yes, there is a spirit of grief it is not the normal grief that one feels within a loss of some kind. No this type of grief wields the captured with an inability to move forward within the natural stages of grief. This spirit links up with hopelessness and produces a chronic state of victimization within its subject. They in turn invite the "Spirits of Bitterness and Rejection," to take up residence which quickly began to plant deep inside my soul the poisonous seeds of bitter root expectations."*

Now let me explain all of this because if you have not been exposed to the truth of demonic oppression and its ability to carry out the assignment of stealing, killing and destroying an individual; all of the above will confuse you. Bitter root expectations are the expectation that people will harm or disappoint you. Within relationships I unknowingly actually began to look for bad things to happen and because of this I started the rejection process of others especially those wanting romantic relationships with me.

I also held tightly onto the mindset that things were always happening to me. I had become a victim in every situation that I perceived as painful. "Why ME?" became my inward mantra that I had no idea was seeping out for others to see. And as each trial hit my life I became entrenched in hopelessness. Now I was not walking around looking like a dark cloud was hovering above me. On the contrary, I wore masks that allowed me to appear happy. I laughed a lot actually too much. I had decided that I would laugh to keep from crying, but crying is what I was doing on the inside all the time. I didn't realize how deeply bound I was until the day I had decided to end it all. I had quit my job due to a temporary physical disability brought on by a car accident, withdrew some money from my bank account, checked into a hotel and neatly placed every pill bottle that I had on the nightstand.

And even as I sit here typing this account I cannot remember how I got to the hotel, or when I had packed all my pills in my purse to bring to work that day. I will offer a bit of background to allow you a look into what led me to that point in my life. At this time my youngest daughter had been taken out of my home because she had placed Lysol in the orange juice container that belonged to my husband. He called the police citing that she had tried to kill him and away they took her. She was 12 at the time. In my mind, I had now completely failed as a mother, by first bringing this abuse in our family by marrying out of fear, and then refusing to face what was happening to my children as I allowed us to remain in it. The Spirit of Suicide who had strategically waited for its opportunity came to the forefront to attempt to carry out its mission of stealing from my children, their mother, killing the future that God had for me, and destroying the opportunity of others being healed by the words of my testimony of deliverance.

Special note- spirits are patient, they wait for the best opportunity to inflict the most damage. Even though many of them enter as far back as within the womb they will not act until their influence can be catastrophic.

On the outside my friends searched desperately for me no one having any idea of where to look. For two days I sat in that hotel room looking at the bottles. I had emptied them and neatly lined the pills. I had turned the television on but muted the sound. On the day that I had decided to carry out the assignment of the enemy a preacher on the television caught my attention. Prompted by the Holy Spirit *(of which I am certain was because of the prayers of my friends)* I turned the sound on and listened to the message being spoken. It was a message of healing and I cried for 24 hours. I cried until my eyes hurt. I cried until my throat burned. I cried until my chest felt like bricks had been resting on it. I had become like Hannah;

***"And she was in bitterness of soul, and prayed to the Lord and wept in anguish."* 1 Samuel 1:10**

The next day I walked into the vestibule of my church and the prayer ministry that I was a part of at the time, took me straight to the prayer room and began to minister to me.

In the following weeks Jesus introduced me to those who would become instrumental in what would be the beginning of the healing and deliverance ministry that would form its operation within my church. Of which I became a healed operating member of. Wounded in the Beloved, there is hope for your suffering. For we have been misled by the doctrine of men to falsely believe that all one needs to do is accept Jesus as Savior and the enemy will no longer bother us and everything that we struggle with will instantly disappear. Some teach that demons cannot harm believers, and that Christians can't have them, but scripture begs to differ-

"Bring the boy here." They brought him. When the demon saw Jesus, it threw the boy into a seizure, causing him to writhe on the ground and foam at the mouth." Mark 9:20

"Now in the synagogue there was a man who was possessed by the foul spirit of a demon; and he cried out with a loud (deep, terrible) cry, Ah, [a] let us alone! What have You to do with us [What have we in common], Jesus of Nazareth? Have You come to destroy us? I know Who You are—the Holy One of God!" **Luke 4:33-34**

"But He turned and said to Peter, "Get behind Me, Satan! You are an offense to Me, for you are not mindful of the things of God, but the things of men." **Matthew 16:23**

"At evening, when the sun had set, they brought to Him all who were sick and those who were demon-possessed. And the whole city was gathered together at the door. Then He healed many who were sick with various diseases, and cast out many demons; and He did not allow the demons to speak, because they knew Him." **Mark 1:32-34**

Sure, it can be argued that within the second scripture the man in the synagogue, believed in God, not Jesus, and how do we know the boy in the first did either? And in the last scriptures who is to say that everyone in that city believed in either The Father or His Son? The real fact is that partial belief is still belief. Whether they believed in The Father or The Son they believed that Jesus had power to heal and deliver and that was enough for God to give them the healing and deliverance they sought. For in all honesty both you and I have operated in this partiality at times. When we believe in one aspect of God and not another, for instance believing that He can and will do abundant things for others but not for ourselves. Or when we believe that He has given us salvation, but that He either can't or won't heal our bodies. Beyond all of that there is no mistaking that Peter definitely believed in God and JESUS and was influenced by the enemy when he spoke what he had in order to cause Jesus to respond in the manner we see there in verse 23. Arguments can be formed out of anything, but what is certain is this- if they are forming around the things of God, then they are most certainly deriving from the enemy to keep us in bondage to him. And it is also certain that you reading this book have at one time in your life confessed Jesus as Lord and Savior and you are right now hurting from some form of abuse.

To you Christian, Believer the below is your current state of being;

"Therefore I will not refrain my mouth; I will speak in the anguish of my spirit; I will complain in the bitterness of my soul." Job 7:11 (KJV).

"Trouble and anguish have taken hold on me: yet thy commandments are my delights. The righteousness of thy testimonies is everlasting: give me understanding, and I shall live." Psalm 119:143-144 (KJV).

RECEIVE YE NOW THIS;

"Be not afraid of sudden fear, neither of the desolation of the wicked when it cometh. For the Lord shall be thy confidence, and shall keep thy foot from being taken." Proverbs 3:25-26 (KJV).

"Who shall separate us from the love of Christ? shall tribulation, or distress, or persecution, or famine, or nakedness, or peril, or sword? As it is written, For thy sake we are killed all the day long; we are accounted as sheep for the slaughter. Nay, in all these things we are more than conquerors through him that loved us. For I am persuaded, that neither death, nor life, nor angels, nor principalities, nor powers, nor things present, nor things to come, Nor

height, nor depth, nor any other creature, shall be able to separate us from the love of God, which is in Christ Jesus our Lord." Romans 8:35-39 (KJV).

And I as a servant of the MOST HIGH proclaim the same words spoken by Jesus, and can be spoken of all who confess Jesus as LORD and accept the ministry of reconciliation that salvation brings. We who are of the Kingdom of God can after receiving the same from HIM boldly profess that;

"The Spirit of the Lord God is upon me, because the Lord has anointed and qualified me to preach the Gospel of good tidings to the meek, the poor, and afflicted; He has sent me to bind up and heal the brokenhearted, to proclaim liberty to the [physical and spiritual] captives and the opening of the prison and of the eyes to those who are bound." Isaiah 61:1

In the wonderful words of a beloved worship song (The Corinthian Song) by Micah Stampley;

"WE ARE VESSELS- FULL OF POWER- WITH A TREASURE FROM THE LORD!"

And we will rise above the tribulations of our time and see the glory of God through Jesus Christ manifest our establishment within the Kingdom of God. For we firmly believe that we have a God who;

"Who comforts (consoles and encourages) us in every trouble (calamity and affliction), so that we may also be able to comfort (console and encourage) those who are in any kind of trouble or distress, with the comfort (consolation and encouragement) with which we ourselves are comforted (consoled and encouraged) by God." 2 Corinthians 1:4

We believe that;

"We are assured and know that [[a] God being a partner in their labor] all things work together and are [fitting into a plan] for good to and for those who love God and are called according to [His] design and purpose." Romans 8:28

By not in any way belittling the harmful experiences that we have endured via abuses we know that,

"For our light, momentary affliction (this slight distress of the passing hour) is ever more and more abundantly preparing and producing and achieving for us an everlasting weight of glory [beyond all measure, excessively surpassing all comparisons and all calculations, a vast

and transcendent glory and blessedness never to cease!]"
2 Corinthians 4:17

Because during these times of great trial and tribulation we have been given this promise from God that,

"I have told you these things, so that in Me you may have [perfect] peace and confidence. In the world you have tribulation and trials and distress and frustration; but be of good cheer [take courage; be confident, certain, undaunted]! For I have overcome the world. [I have deprived it of power to harm you and have conquered it for you.]" John 16:33

Clean House

"So clean house! Make a clean sweep of malice and pretense, envy and hurtful talk. You've had a taste of God. Now, like infants at the breast, drink deep of God's pure kindness. Then you'll grow up mature and whole in God."

1 Peter 2:1-3

This chapter is devoted to scripture that will help you maintain your deliverance to keep a clean house. As you take the voyage into the deep hurts of your past and present circumstances an emptying is going to take place and wherever something is plucked out something else has to take its place to prevent the following from occurring;

"When a defiling evil spirit is expelled from someone, it drifts along through the desert looking for an oasis, some unsuspecting soul it can bedevil. When it doesn't find anyone, it says, 'I'll go back to my old haunt.' On return it finds the person spotlessly clean, but vacant. It then runs out and rounds up seven other spirits more evil than itself

and they all move in, whooping it up. That person ends up far worse off than if he'd never gotten cleaned up in the first place."

Mathew 12:43-44

So to you my fellow sisters and brothers in Christ place in the excavated places these life restoring Words of God;

"Present yourselves as building stones for the construction of a sanctuary vibrant with life, in which you'll serve as holy priests offering Christ-approved lives up to God." 1 Peter2:5

"But you are the ones chosen by God, chosen for the high calling of priestly work, chosen to be a holy people, God's instruments to do his work and speak out for him, to tell others of the night-and-day difference he made for you—from nothing to something, from rejected to accepted." 1Peter 2:9-10

"You shall establish yourself in righteousness (rightness, in conformity with God's will and order): you shall be far from even the thought of oppression or destruction, for you shall not fear, and from terror, for it shall not come near you." Isaiah 54:14

"But no weapon that is formed against you shall prosper, and every tongue that shall rise against you in judgment you shall show to be in the wrong. This [peace, righteousness, security, triumph over opposition] is the heritage of the servants of the Lord [those in whom the ideal Servant of the Lord is reproduced]; this is the righteousness or the vindication which they obtain from Me [this is that which I impart to them as their justification], says the Lord." **Isaiah 54:17**

"For the weapons of your warfare are not physical [weapons of flesh and blood], but they are mighty before God for the overthrow and destruction of strongholds." **2Corinthians 10:4**

"Lift up over all the [covering] shield of [a] saving faith, upon which you can quench all the flaming missiles of the wicked [one]. And take the helmet of salvation and the sword that the Spirit [b] wields, which is the Word of God." **Ephesians 6:16-17**

"For God did not give me a spirit of timidity (of cowardice, of craven and cringing and fawning fear), but [He has given me a spirit] of power and of love and of calm and well-balanced mind and discipline and self-control." **2Timothy 1:7**

"You prepare a table before me in the presence of my enemies. You anoint my head with oil; my [brimming] cup runs over. Surely or only goodness, mercy, and unfailing love shall follow me all the days of my life, and through the length of my days the house of the Lord [and His presence] shall be my dwelling place." **Psalm 23:5-6**

"And the Lord shall make you the head, and not the tail; and you shall be above only, and you shall not be beneath, if you heed the commandments of the Lord your God which I command you this day and are watchful to do them." **Deuteronomy 28:13**

"In Him I have redemption (deliverance and salvation) through His blood, the remission (forgiveness) of my offenses (shortcomings and trespasses), in accordance with the riches and the generosity of His gracious favor," **Ephesians 1:7**

"It is through Him that we have received grace (God's unmerited favor) and [our] apostleship to promote obedience to the faith and make disciples for His name's sake among all the nations, And this includes you, called of Jesus Christ and invited [as you are] to belong to Him." **Romans 1:5-6**

"By which have been given to us exceedingly great and precious promises, that through these you may be partakers of the divine nature, having escaped the corruption that is in the world through lust. But also for this very reason, giving all diligence, add to your faith virtue, to virtue knowledge, to knowledge self-control, to self-control perseverance, to perseverance godliness, to godliness brotherly kindness, and to brotherly kindness love." **2 Peter 1:4-7**

"Finally, brethren, whatever things are true, whatever things are noble, whatever things are just, whatever things are pure, whatever things are lovely, whatever things are of good report, if there is any virtue and if there is anything praiseworthy—meditate on these things." **Philippians 4:8**

Arise In Victory

"But thanks be to God, Who gives us the victory [making us conquerors] through our Lord Jesus Christ."

1 Corinthians 15:57

This chapter has been both the easiest and the hardest to pen. Because it is ongoing, being called to arise in victory is a clarion call that has no end. The Father who sits in heaven has proclaimed within His divine word that **ALL VICTORY** belongs unto those that trust **in HIM**.

In many areas of my life I am just learning what this means for me. As I sat pondering the realization that all has not been attained, as I desire in Christ, I began to wonder should I even be writing this book. And then I heard;

"That is the exact reason that you have been commissioned to write it. Because you have finally come to understand that a relationship with Me is an ever evolving one. And just because you have made great strides in some

areas there are and will be until My Son comes again, areas within you that require My strong hand of deliverance. Thus the subtitle of this book "Doesn't Have to Stay In this House." For indeed My people are in need of much healing and much deliverance and often they err in stopping the process of the work that I have begun in them believing that in that moment that is all the work that I desire to compete in them. There is always more. More that you do not understand, more that I have not yet revealed, more for you to reconcile in Me. More of Me that I want to make known in you. For I am the GOD of Exceedingly, and Abundantly."

And with that being said, this will be the shortest chapter in the entire book for the remaining work is between YOU and HIM. I will end with this-

He longs to give you the ability to

<u>ARISE IN VICTORY.</u>

FOREVER!!!

About the Author

Deidra Saddler is currently an Ordained Elder of Kingdom Apostolic Church International of Chicago. It is within this ministry, she is one of the co-leaders of intercessory prayer ministry known as The Mishmar Ministry (Mishmar means "Watch" in Hebrew) and a co-leader of the Alpha & Omega Deliverance Teams. Deidra has simultaneously been a dedicated member of Precious Stone Ministries an apostolic ministry that has been commissioned to empower the body of Christ by helping ministries build deliverance teams. Through the prompting of the Holy Spirit, Deidra has established a drama ministry entitled, "In2MeSeeBreakthru," where she creates and acts out Holy Spirit inspired dramatizations." Her greatest desire is to create a traveling drama team that will go wherever God sends ministering in plays that reveal the works of the enemy, deeply hidden pain, and allows healing encounters to be experienced by those who are in attendance. An avid writer, she is walking out in faith in the realm of publication as she writes books that speak the truth and help to heal the wounded. "I delight in the freedom of believers in CHRIST JESUS!"

More From Faith Walk Publishing

Thank you for taking time to read one of our books. We pray that it has blessed you. If this book has touched you in way, please take time out to review the book.

Also

Check out some of our other titles!

www.faithwalkpublishing.com

www.ingramcontent.com/pod-product-compliance
Lightning Source LLC
Chambersburg PA
CBHW021136300426
44113CB00006B/448